Journey Of Stones

A Sermon Series
For Lent And Easter

Steven Molin

CSS Publishing Company, Inc., Lima, Ohio

JOURNEY OF STONES

For more information about CSS Publishing Company resources, visit our website at
www.csspub.com or e-mail us at custserv@csspub.com or call (800) 241-4056.

ISBN 0-7880-1932-5   PRINTED IN U.S.A.

To Charlotte Johnson,
thank you for encouraging me to write

Table Of Contents

Foreword

These sermons promise a journey — a journey of stones. Befitting Lent, Pastor Steve Molin takes us on a journey of prayerful and honest repentance — a powerful, life-changing journey that calls for private and corporate expression. But the sermons will also lead us on a journey of celebration, of grace, of awe at the miracle of the empty tomb and the promise of life.

As sermons, what you are about to read are powerful invitations to amendment of life; as devotional readings, they will encourage personal reflection and acknowledgment of the need for God's mercies. Each contains a call to place a stone at the foot of the cross — to lay at the feet of our Savior all of those things which separate us from him.

Each sermon tells a story. Pastor Molin is one of the best sermon storytellers I've heard. But each sermon and every story also teaches a biblical text. These are sermons grounded in the living Word of God, in the history of God's people, and in the call to be faithful Christians in this age. This *Journey of Stones* is a journey for God's people; a journey which ends with the joyous invitation to be free, to be alive in Christ!

Along the way, we will confess our faith, we will weep with sorrow, we will tell the truth about ourselves, and we will eat and drink bread and wine. We will stand together at the foot of the cross, lay our stones — and our sins — down, and leave in wonder. We will together journey through Holy Week and together proclaim the resurrection.

Steve Molin has been my pastor for a few years; enough years so that I know his life speaks what his words say. As he preached these sermons at Our Savior's Lutheran Church in Stillwater, Minnesota, we laid our stones, our sins, our tears, at the foot of the cross. Pastor Steve's words and actions led us to the cross; the Holy Spirit met us there and we were changed.

On Easter Sunday, we were ready — really ready — to announce together the Good News, "He is risen!" We'd laid our sins at the cross and now, behold! They were gone! This Good News is for all of us. Thanks be to God!

Glenndy Sculley
Bishop's Associate
Minneapolis Area Synod

Introduction

As worshipers enter the sanctuary, they are met by a wheelbarrow filled with small white landscape rocks, and a sign which reads: **Take a stone into worship with you.** As each sermon unfolds, the stones which people hold become symbolic of the sins of our lives. As each sermon ends, worshipers are encouraged to pass by the large timber cross at the front of the sanctuary and lay their stones (their sin) at its base. Questions are provided for thought and discussion as worshipers leave the sanctuary. (**Note:** the stones for the Good Friday service should have a simple black cross painted on them.)

On Easter Sunday, the stones have been removed! As "someone rolled the stone away," so too someone has removed their stones of sin on Easter! What we could not do for ourselves, Someone else did for us. And that is the ultimate Easter message on this Journey of Stones. As people leave worship on Easter Sunday, each person receives another stone — this one a prayer pebble — inscribed with the simple truth of Easter: *Alive!*

Written In Stone
Exodus 32:1-24

Dear friends in Christ, grace, mercy, and peace, from God our Father and his Son, our Lord and Savior, Jesus Christ. Amen.

Have you ever made a promise, and then gone back on your word? I'll bet you have; and I'm not speaking of the minor agreements that we make to one another every day. Phrases like "I promise I'll brush my teeth at Billy's sleepover." Or "I promise to take out the garbage on Friday morning." Rather, I refer to the agreements that have significant and far-reaching consequences for our lives. Promises that, if we break them, turn our world upside down. Let me show you what I mean.

Mike and Helen were a couple very much in love. They dated for more than two years, and then decided to get married. Following months of planning and preparation, Mike and Helen stood in front of their pastor and hundreds of family and friends on a Saturday afternoon, and they made some promises to each other. A kiss sealed their commitment, the applause of their witnesses affirmed it, and they lived happily ever after. For about a year.

On their first anniversary, Mike discovered that Helen had been unfaithful. You don't need to hear the details, except to know that Helen did not keep her end of their agreement. Now Mike was standing before his wife, holding in his hands the covenant they had signed on their wedding day. He began to read it out loud:

> ***Question:*** *Will you love him, comfort him, honor and keep him?*
> ***Answer:*** *Yes.*
>
> ***Question:*** *Will you care for him for richer or poorer, in sickness and in health?*
> ***Answer:*** *Yes.*

Question: Will you be faithful to him as long as you both shall live?
Answer: Yes.

With that, Mike tore their wedding covenant into tiny pieces and threw them into the air. And they never spoke again, except through their attorneys. Not ever. You see, when a covenant is broken, it is not easily repaired. When a promise is made, it is like a gleaming crystal vase. But when a promise is broken, the pieces lie shattered on the floor.

The story of God's covenant with you and me goes back more than 4,000 years, when a leader named Moses was called high on a mountain to meet with God face-to-face. Moses was already a hero, having been used by God to bring the people of Israel out of slavery and into a land of their own. Now God was offering these same people a promise, a relationship that was so special the people of Israel could only be called "chosen." These are the words that God used:

> *If you will obey my voice, and keep my covenant, then you shall be my special treasure among all peoples ... you shall be to me a kingdom of priests and a holy nation.*

When Moses brought God's offer to the people of Israel, the people were ecstatic. They immediately agreed to obey God's commands. "We will do it!" they shouted. "Everything the Lord has spoken we will do, and we will be obedient." So Moses went back up to the top of the mountain and sealed the deal. It was not a kiss between lovers. It wasn't the applause of the angels. It was contract time, and God's expectations would be written in stone.

It's an interesting phrase, isn't it? "Written in stone." We use that idiom yet today to describe something that is secure and long-lasting, in fact, something that is to be permanent. That is exactly what God intended the Ten Commandments to be — a covenant that would last forever. With his own hands, God cut the tablets. With his own fingers, God engraved the words. God's love for his people was written in stone.

But the problem was, it took God forty days. The people of Israel, who waited impatiently, finally began to get restless. They figured Moses wasn't coming back. And then Aaron had a bright idea! "Quickly" he told the people, "take off your jewelry; your rings, your bracelets, and your earrings. Let's make a golden calf, a god for us to worship that we can see and touch and believe in." And so they did.

By the time Moses came down the mountain, a party was in progress. People were singing and dancing and drinking and playing "ring around the rosy" at an altar with a golden god upon it. And Moses was furious! In anger, he threw down the tablets of God and they shattered into a thousand pieces. It was not a symbolic gesture; it was a sign that the covenant was ended. The deal was off! A special relationship no longer existed between God and the people that God loved.

In my mind's eye, I see the people of Israel, picking up small pieces of the tablets, with thoughts of what might have been. Holding these broken rocks in their hands — some of which still held the handwriting of God — must have filled them with grief and guilt and shame. It wasn't Moses who shattered the covenant, that much they knew. It was their own sinful, selfish lives and the breaking of the promise which they had made to God.

Four thousand years is a long, long time. It's long enough to remove the guilt that accompanies a broken promise. And it is certainly long enough to relieve us from feeling responsible for others disobeying God. What were those foolish Israelites thinking? How could they so blatantly and so intentionally break God's laws? But then, the honest ones among us realize that we wouldn't have acted any differently than they did, because we break God's laws all the time. Don't we? Don't we?

The Ten Commandments were not merely intended for the people of Israel, circa 1000 B.C. They're written in stone, remember? The Laws of God are timeless, changeless expectations. But you and I so often choose to violate them, or ignore them, or rewrite them to fit our own circumstances, and then we assume that God will look the other way.

We're told by God that he alone wants to be our God. Author Leith Anderson suggests that everybody has a center of life; it is that thing which is most important to us, and it controls everything about us.[1] Well, if God is at our center, then that will be obvious by the way we live. But if our god is, say, wealth or power or popularity or our spouse or our children or our hobbies ... then we have broken that which was written in stone.

We're told by God to honor our father and mother, and most of the time we do. But there are those times when we fail. "My old man says I have to mow the lawn." "My mom thinks I'm at the library studying, but what she doesn't know won't hurt her." "My parents are the stupidest people I know. Oh, I hate them!" And again, we have broken what was written in stone.

We're told by God that we are not supposed to lie, and we say we agree. But a recent poll revealed that 91 percent of Americans lie regularly, and only 31 percent believe that honesty is the best policy.[2] Whenever we lie, or whenever we fail to tell the truth, we have broken that which was written in stone.

We're told by God that we should not steal, and we say we will obey. But even religious people fudge on their income tax forms and think nothing of it. And academic cheating has reached epidemic proportions on our campuses, but students don't see the problem. "No blood — no foul," they say. And again, we have broken that which was written in stone.

We're told by God that we shouldn't commit adultery, and we think that's a good suggestion. But since 1960, there has been a 400 percent increase in illegitimate births in America. Ninety-five percent of the couples I marry are sexually active before their wedding day. And if you want to get technical, Jesus was quoted as saying, "Anyone who divorces his wife and marries another commits adultery." Jesus also said, "Anyone who looks at a person with lust in his heart has already committed adultery." It is written in stone, but apparently it just doesn't matter.

The issue here is not that we have broken the Commandments, but rather, that we have become a broken people. We are guilty and ashamed of the things we have done and said. We have hurt others, hurt ourselves, and hurt God. Ultimately we come to this realization: we need a Savior who will save us from ourselves. The season of Lent is our time to ask God to forgive our foolishness.

Tonight, you hold in your hands pieces of stone. Notice that they are not smooth stones; rather, their edges are sharp and jagged, as if broken. We have a choice tonight — and every Wednesday during the season of Lent — as to what to do with those stones. We can hang on to them as a painful reminder of our sin, and it will continue to make us bitter, broken people. Or we can let them go; we can lay them at the foot of the cross, and ask God to give us another chance.

Before you leave this evening, I invite you to leave your broken stone with Jesus Christ. Thanks be to God. Amen.

---

1. Leith Anderson, *Winning the Values War in a Changing Culture*, 1994, Bethany House Publishers.

2. James Patterson and Peter Kim, *The Day America Told the Truth*, 1991, Prentice Hall Press.

Discussion Questions

1. What promises are most frequently broken in the world today? Which promise is most frequently broken by me?

2. What is it about the gods of this world that are so attractive to us?

3. What did the pastor mean when we were referred to as "broken people"?

Rejected Stones
Psalm 118; Mark 12:1-2

Dear friends in Christ, grace, mercy, and peace, from God our Father and his Son, our Lord and Savior, Jesus Christ. Amen.

It's a terrible thing to be rejected. To be told in word or attitude or action that we're unacceptable or unworthy or unnecessary is a terrible thing indeed. And I'm wondering tonight if that has ever happened to you. Have you ever been turned down by your college of choice, or not chosen for the job of your dreams, or not selected by that special boy or girl? It's a terrible thing, to be rejected.

I have discovered over a lifetime that rejection can propel us in one of two directions. It can either cause in us resilience and a determination to succeed, or it can make us bitter, resentful, and jaded. Rejection can transform us into caring, sensitive, and compassionate human beings, or it can leave us cold, judgmental, and angry.

As a case in point, let me share with you the words of Dr. James Dobson, written about one who was rejected, and see if you can guess who it was. Dobson writes:

> *His life began with all the classic handicaps and disadvantages. His mother had been married three times; his father died a few months before he was born. His mother gave him no affection, no love, no discipline, and no training in those early years. She even forbade him to call her at work. Other children would have nothing to do with him. At the age of thirteen, a school psychologist commented that the boy probably didn't know the meaning of the word "love." During adolescence, the girls would have nothing to do with him and he fought with the boys.*
> *As a young adult, he failed academically and then dropped out of high school. He joined the Marines but*

17

the other Marines laughed at him and made fun of him. In time, he was court-martialed and thrown out of the military. When he eventually married, his wife belittled him, ridiculed his sexual impotence, and ultimately divorced him.

Finally, in silence, he pleaded no more. No one wanted him. No one had ever wanted him. He was perhaps the most rejected man of our time. Then, one day, he arose, went to the garage and took down a rifle he had hidden there, and brought it to his newly-acquired job at a book storage building. And shortly after noon on November 22, 1963, he sent two shells crashing into the head of President John Fitzgerald Kennedy.[1]

That "most rejected man of our time" was, of course, Lee Harvey Oswald.

In Old Testament times, the Jews were a rejected people. All the powerful and mighty nations of the world looked at them and laughed; they dismissed Israel as an unimportant and dishonored people. But God had a different idea. In the Psalm, which we read a few minutes ago, God spoke of the Jews as stones ... important stones. "The same stone which the builders rejected has become the chief cornerstone," the psalmist said.

You should know that, in ancient times, in the days before laser beams and electronic levels, the cornerstone was more than just a place on which to write the date of the building. It was the most important stone in the entire structure. It alone would establish a building's ground level. It alone assured that the foundation would be solid. The cornerstone ensured that all the other stones would be kept in line, straight and level and secure. God said that the people of Israel would be the world's cornerstone, that ultimately they would be powerful and respected and honored. Well, they may have been God's chosen stones, but they were stones rejected by the rest of the world. That's what the words of the psalmist mean.

When Jesus is telling his parable in today's Gospel lesson, he is speaking to those same Jews, the ones who were chosen by God but rejected by the world. They were supposed to be cornerstones.

They were supposed to be the moral and ethical and religious compass of humanity, but they became compromised along the way. God had provided them with everything they would need to be content and happy in this world; their only responsibility was to be faithful and righteous. When God sent prophets and priests to remind the Jews of their responsibility, the Jews rejected them, they ridiculed them, and in some cases, they even killed the prophets. And through the voice of the parable, Jesus suggests to the Jews that they would even kill God's Son if he were to come. Guess what happened? Now Jesus becomes the cornerstone. He becomes the most important stone in the church. He sets the moral standard. He alone holds the church together. Only he is the foundation upon which the Kingdom of God rests. And he was rejected by the very people who were supposed to receive him. Now the words of the psalmist have come full circle, when Jesus says, "Have you not read this scripture: 'The stone which the builders rejected, this became the chief cornerstone.' "

Well, it didn't really come full circle; that doesn't happen until we realize that we too have rejected Jesus as the cornerstone of our lives. We can criticize the Jews all we want to, but we must come to terms with the fact that we too have not let Christ set the moral and ethical standard for us. We say he is, but we fail to follow his call upon our lives. For the most part, Jesus is not the cornerstone that holds us up, but rather the millstone that drags us down. His expectations are too great, we say, so we reject his claim upon our lives and do things our way.

I believe it was Saint Augustine who created the pyramid of priorities, and each of us has one. Here is how it works: we list the six most important things in our life. Maybe they would be *family*, *money, reputation, job, God*, and *health*. But when you're asked to take two away, what would you have left? Perhaps *family, job, God*, and *health*. Now eliminate two more. You see the dilemma, don't you? Augustine says that when you get down to that one final thing ... that thing that you say is most valuable ... that becomes the god of your life. That becomes the cornerstone.

You say, "Well, Pastor, we're not ever faced with those sorts of choices, so it's really a silly exercise." I disagree. I think we're faced with those choices on a daily basis, but we have become so accustomed to rationalizing our behavior, we don't see it as rejecting Jesus. It doesn't matter what you call it; that's exactly what it is.

We are soon coming upon the anniversary of the shooting at Columbine High School in Littleton, Colorado. "Columbine" has become synonymous with the anger and angst and disillusionment that seems to permeate our culture today. Two teenage boys — themselves rejected by their peers — went on a tragic rampage. One of the people they encountered in the library that afternoon was a young woman by the name of Cassie Burnall. With a gun pointed directly at her face, she was asked if she believed in God. She could have said, "No," and lived. She could have rejected the One whom she believed to be the Cornerstone of her life, and the shooter would have gone to someone else. She said, "Yes." In fact, that is now the title of the book written by Cassie's mom: *She Said, "Yes."* And they killed her.

Few of us, if any, will ever have to take that kind of stand. But our conflicts of conscience present themselves in everyday settings like telling the truth on our income tax forms or not; being faithful in our marriage or not; giving our children role models they can emulate or not; having integrity in every business dealing or not. These are the ways that we reject Jesus in this present age.

Once again tonight, you hold in your hands a stone. It's an important stone — perhaps the most important of stones — because it is symbolic of Jesus as the cornerstone of our lives. Maybe you don't need to lay this stone at the foot of the cross tonight, as indication of the times you have rejected Jesus. Maybe you will take that stone home with you. In your honest introspection, you believe that you have not rejected Jesus in your daily living. Then please take the stone home. But I know what I must do. (*Pastor places stone at foot of cross.*)

---

1. Dr. James Dobson, *Hide or Seek: How to Build Self-Esteem in Your Child*, 1974, Fleming H. Revell Company.

Discussion Questions

1. Jesus implied that he was rejected. "Rejected" is a strong word. Have you ever been rejected (job application, romance, athletic team, group of friends, etc.)? How did that make you feel?

2. In what ways do people reject God today?

3. Jesus asked this question at the end of the parable: "What will the vineyard owner do when he comes back?" Assuming that Jesus is the vineyard owner, how would you answer that question?

Sticks And Stones
John 8:1-12

Dear friends in Christ, grace, mercy, and peace, from God our Father and his Son, our Lord and Savior, Jesus Christ. Amen.

This evening I need the help of the children in our congregation. You may stay seated where you are, but I need your help in remembering some of the playground phrases that you might chant with your friends, or even say to your enemies, as children your age sometimes do. When you hear me begin a familiar one, just join in and say it with me. The louder the better!

Liar, liar, pants on fire. Nose as long as a telephone wire.

How about this one: *John and Linda, sittin' in a tree, K-I-S-S-I-N-G. First comes love, then comes marriage. Then comes Linda with a baby carriage.*

Maybe your parents will have to help you with this one: it's old — ancient — and you may not have heard of it before: *Made you look. Made you look. Made you buy a penny-book.* I'm not even sure what a "penny-book" is, but I am certain that you can't buy it for a penny anymore.

We want a pitcher, not a belly-itcher.

And then there's this one: *Sticks and stones may break my bones, but words can never hurt me.*

Most of the playground phrases of children have a ring of truth to them ... except that last one. "Sticks and stones may break my bones, but words can never hurt me." We know, from our own experience, that criticism can hurt us deeply. Yet we tell our children otherwise, whenever the other kids are being cruel. "Just ignore them," we say. "Don't pay any attention to what the others say. Remember, 'Sticks and stones may break your bones, but words can never hurt you.' " But we know it's not true. Someone once wrote a more accurate idiom that goes this way: "Sticks and stones may break my bones, but words can sting like anything." And you know that's true! You know it's true.

A teenage girl walks by a group of ninth grade boys, and one of them whispers in an audible voice, "Hey, Lisa's getting a little chunky, don't you think? Oink! Oink! Oink!" Of course, Lisa laughs out loud as she hurries by, and then she heads off to the nearest restroom and melts into a million tears. In the future, she'll pay countless visits to that restroom, but now it's to purge and vomit the salad and rice cakes she just ate in the school cafeteria. You've seen it happen and so have I.

Or a father carelessly calls his college-aged son "lazy" or "stupid" or "clumsy" or "irresponsible." The boy doesn't care; he just slinks off to his bedroom and turns up the stereo, but inside, a little piece of him dies of humiliation. "Sticks and stones may break my bones, but words can sting like anything." And we do it all the time. And sometimes, we even do it on purpose.

The late Pastor Mark Jerstad, former president of Good Samaritan Society, once remarked that the tongue is the most powerful muscle in the human body. "It only weighs a quarter pound," he said, "but in a single moment, it can destroy a person's reputation or demolish their sense of self-worth." And it's been that way for years.

Jesus was teaching early one morning in the synagogue, when the Pharisees brought in a woman who had been caught committing adultery. Imagine that! Right in the middle of conducting worship, and they drag this woman into the sanctuary for trial. Scripture doesn't say she was naked, but I presume she was. If she was caught "in the very act of adultery," I doubt that they gave her time to get dressed before hauling her off to be executed!

"Master, this woman was caught in the very act of sleeping with a man who is not her husband. Our Law teaches that a woman such as this be stoned to death. What do you say?" "A woman such as this. A woman such as this!" The label must have stung as it landed on her ears, but just in case she missed the charge, the onlookers piled on the evidence. "She's nothing but a slut! She's a whore! She's trash! We say stone her to death." But there's more than one way to stone someone. In fact, they didn't even need to stone her. She was already dying a slow and painful death ... there

... in the church ... in front of her community and in the presence of Jesus.

It's been said that religious people are the only army who ever shoot their wounded, and that's what is unfolding here. Two hundred hands picked up their stones of judgment. Two hundred eyes gawked at a woman such as this. But one pair of eyes refused to stare. Jesus looked down at the ground and began writing in the dirt. He refused to add to the woman's humiliation. Jesus refused to condemn her, though he was the only one gathered who was qualified to do so.

"Here's my judgment," Jesus announced to the self-righteous crowd. "Whoever has never sinned, you may cast the first stone." If you're perfect, let 'em fly! If your life is without sin, you can start the stoning. It's no accident that the older Pharisees were the first to leave. As we age, it seems we become more aware of our shortcomings, and more honest about our own failures. Pretty soon, even the youngest, most zealous Pharisees had dropped their stones at Jesus' feet and left the temple. According to the rules, the woman deserved to die. She was, after all, caught in the very act! But this time, compassion won out. This time, love was more powerful than justice. "Is there no one left to condemn you?" Jesus asked. "No, sir," the woman replied. "Then neither do I condemn you. Go and sin no more."

If this story were to be told today, I fear that we would be the Pharisees. We, who insulate ourselves from the real sinners of this world, by our pious speech and our self-righteous attitudes; it is our hands that would be filled with stones. And we would aim them at anyone who did not think, or did not act, or did not speak, or did not believe the way we do. Literally, the word *Pharisee* means "people who have separated themselves." And don't we do that? Don't we take pride in the fact that we're not like those who steal, or those who are addicted, or those who can't make marriage work, or those whose children are ne'er do well, or those whose significant other is the same gender. C'mon, admit it: we're better than them! We don't do the things that people such as these do, so we have earned the right to cast stones at them. You see, that's what the Pharisees thought ... and Jesus said they were wrong.

He did not say that the sinner was innocent ... in fact, he told her to go and sin no more. But he did imply that she deserved the compassion — not the wrath — of those who wanted to stone her.

Two thousand years after the fact, we readily admit that Jesus was right, that the woman deserved a second chance. And yet we are so harshly critical of people just like her in our day, people who make mistakes and break the rules. We can absolve her of her centuries-old indiscretion, but we condemn the 21st-century sinners. We can forgive the adulterous woman, but we do not forgive an adulterous president. We resent the actions of the Pharisees in Jesus' day, but we have carried on their tradition of judgment and scorn and punishment for those who get caught in the very act today. Loaded with stones ... or words ... or attitudes of self-righteousness, we are proud to cast the first stone. In short, we have met the Pharisees and they are us! Rigid. Religious. Unbending. And wrong.

There is another way, and Lent is a good time to consider it. Robert Schuller was invited to an African American church in the deep South, to observe the anniversary of the Emancipation Proclamation. When he stood up to preach to a sea of black faces, Schuller was overcome with emotion. Here were the great-grandsons and great-granddaughters of slaves, many of whom had been humiliated and abused. Though he tried to speak, the words would not come, and Schuller spent several minutes at the pulpit ... weeping. Finally, the host pastor joined Dr. Schuller at the podium, he himself now crying. The African American pastor put his arm around the white preacher and said, "Dr. Schuller, in this church, no one weeps alone."

That is compassion. That is tenderness. And that is the gospel. The stones you hold this night — both real and imagined — have perhaps already been targeted for someone. Those who have never sinned may take them with you. The rest of us are invited to lay them at the foot of the cross and be given a second chance. Thanks be to God. Amen.

Discussion Questions

1. Pastor said, "There is more than one way to stone someone." In the context of where you spend most of your time (school, work, family, circle of friends) how do people throw stones at one another?

2. Who do you think was the most surprised at the words that Jesus spoke to the woman ... the woman, or the Pharisees, or the disciples? Why?

3. Do we need people in the world like the Pharisees, who would make sure that the rest of us live and act properly? Who, do you think, functions in that capacity for you?

Hearts Of Stone
Luke 11:37-52

A mother prepared a dinner of fish and chips for her family one evening, and because it was her five-year-old son's favorite meal, she asked him to say grace. They bowed their heads, and David began, "Dear God, thank you for these pancakes. Amen." When he finished, his mother said to him, "David, you knew we were having fish for dinner; why did you thank God for pancakes?" "Because," David said, "I just wanted to see if God was paying attention."

Sometimes pastors wonder if their congregation is paying attention. Especially during Lent — when the journey is long and the messages are harsh — it is tempting to tune out and think about spring or Resurrection or Easter hams. But again tonight, we must focus on our sin ... and the Savior who came to love us. May God give us perseverance as we travel this road together. Let us pray ...

> *God of grace, we are a weary people. Ash Wednesday is three weeks behind us; Good Friday is three weeks ahead. Give us strength for the journey, and just enough faith to carry us to Calvary and the cross. In the Name of the Crucified One we pray. Amen.*

Dear friends in Christ, grace, mercy, and peace, from God our Father and his Son, our Lord and Savior, Jesus Christ. Amen.

The question is: Who in the world did these scribes and Pharisees think they were? These religious men of means of first-century Judaism, who continually confronted Jesus with roadblocks of reason, while Jesus confronted them with building blocks of justice and love. Who did they think they were?

Simplistically, they can be described this way. The Pharisees were religious purists who very carefully observed every aspect of Jewish Law. If the Law called for a fast, they began their fast early and stayed late. If the Law called for a tithe, they gave a tithe *and an offering*, and everybody knew it. You see, that was another characteristic of the Pharisees; they portrayed themselves as better than the rank and file folks. Even their label suggests it: "The Pharisees: men who separated themselves." They refused to associate with the sinners around them, to the point where they actually attached blinders on the sides of their heads so they didn't have to look at the sinners. Because of this, they frequently ran into walls and posts, and thus sarcastically came to be known as "the bleeding Pharisees."

The scribes were associated with the Pharisees as lawyers and legal counselors. They were the experts on Jewish Law. They determined how a law ought to be observed, and how it might also be avoided. They even crafted escape clauses that enabled them to do work on the Sabbath. Listen to the words that were written:

> *To carry a burden is forbidden. He who carries anything, whether it be in his right hand, or in his left hand, or in his bosom, or on his shoulder is guilty. But he who carries anything on the back of his hand, or with his foot, or with his mouth, or with his elbow, or with his ear, or with his hair, or with his money bag turned upside down, or between his money bag and his shirt, or in the fold of his shirt, or in his shoe, or in his sandal is not guilty, because he does not carry it in the usual way of carrying it.*

This is the way in which the scribes and the Pharisees observed and avoided the Law. And then they condemned anyone who did not do it their way. And all of this was done in the name of religion, you see.

And then one day, Jesus came to town; he came to eat dinner in the home of a well-known Pharisee. Jesus didn't wash his hands before beginning the meal. Oh, not that his hands were dirty; that wasn't the issue. Hand washing was a ceremony ... a big ritual before the meal, and between each course ... but Jesus didn't observe it. When he was asked about it, Jesus became angry — uncharacteristically angry. Jesus exploded at his dinner host. "You

Pharisees are all alike!" Jesus said. "You take great care in washing the outside — for appearance sake — but meanwhile the inside remains filthy." And it was then that Jesus began his list of warnings ... his list of "woes" if you will. The first three are directed at the Pharisees.

"Woe to you Pharisees," Jesus said. "You give ten percent of everything. Wheat, barley, mint, everything! But you fail to love God, and you fail to treat people with justice. Shame on you!"

"Woe to you Pharisees," Jesus continued, "because you always take the very best seats in the synagogue, in the very front row, and you sit there, not so you can see ... but so that you can be seen! Shame on you."

"And woe to you Pharisees, for you tell people that if they touch a gravestone — even by accident — they will be unclean. And yet you Pharisees are walking gravestones! Your faith is dead and you don't even know it!"

At this point, a certain scribe stood up and addressed Jesus. "Teacher, when you speak to the Pharisees like this, you hurt our feelings." To which Jesus replied, "Well, woe to you, too! Woe to you scribes; you make rules for others to follow, and then you invent ways for yourselves to escape them. Woe to you scribes, because the only prophets you like are dead prophets. When the living prophets come to you, you turn them away. Woe to you scribes, for you have made the Scriptures a book of riddles that only confuse and confound the people. Shame on you, too!"

The common thread in all of these woes is the fact that the scribes and the Pharisees wanted to keep their hands on the religious gate of entrance. They wanted to determine what the rules were. They wanted to decide who met the rules and who broke them. They wanted to preserve the church the way it was for them — the way they always liked it. They used their own lives as a yardstick to measure themselves and others. And that is why Jesus was so brutal in his attack of them.

If there is one comforting fact in this story, it is that Jesus was not denouncing scribes and Pharisees, that is, religious people, *per se*. He was condemning their religious piety. He was denouncing their legalism. He was criticizing their pride ... especially when it became religious pride.

The contemporary application of this text is both subtle and potentially painful, and it is this: If we met a Pharisee on the street today, he or she would probably look a lot like us. Isn't it we who want to determine what the religious rules ought to be? Isn't our individual Christian experience now the yardstick by which we measure religious people? You see, it is possible to have Lutheran Pharisees, or Catholic Pharisees, or Baptist or Methodist or Presbyterian Pharisees. It happens whenever people are so convinced that their way is the right way, that they dismiss others as being wrong.

I'm not talking about doctrine here — we need doctrine; I am talking about tolerance for disagreement. I'm not talking about structure here — every church needs structure; I am talking about style. How do we care for people who do not readily fit into our congregation's structure? Love them or hate them? Dismiss them or coexist with them? Jesus proved, rather emphatically on the cross, that love is more important than rules. Jesus proclaimed that people are more important than programs. Compassion is more important than protocol. But Pharisees of every age disagree, so rather than embrace the people Jesus embraces, the Pharisees choose to fiddle with the fine print, and it takes our focus away from mission and places it on minutia.

Sociologist Anthony Campolo once described the greatest criticism he ever received while speaking in a church. Standing before the piously-dressed, religious-sounding congregation, Campolo announced, "Tonight in West Africa, 6,000 people will die of starvation and you don't give a shit." The people gasped, but Campolo continued, "And right now, you are more concerned about the fact that I said shit in your pulpit than you are about the 6,000 people who will die." And perhaps you are too?

The point is, Campolo's hearers didn't get it. And Jesus' hearers didn't get it either. On the contrary, they resented being scolded. Their hearts were hardened and they responded with ridicule and criticism and rejection. Do you recall how tonight's Gospel story ended?

When Jesus left that place, the scribes and the Phari-
sees began to criticize him bitterly and ask him ques-
tions about many things, trying to lay traps for him
and catch him saying something wrong.

Once a heart has turned to stone, it is difficult to soften it again. Sometimes it takes humility to turn the heart around. Sometimes it takes confession. Why, sometimes it even takes a death. Whatever it takes for you, I encourage you to lay your heart at the foot of the cross tonight, and let the softening process begin. Or woe to us! Woe to us, indeed. Thanks be to God. Amen.

Discussion Questions

1. What religious rules in our society today are rather foolish or useless? If you were "in charge" would you suspend these rules?

2. How do you think Jesus truly felt about the Pharisees? (Love? Anger? Frustration?) Now ... how do you think Jesus feels about you?

3. Tonight, the pastor said, "Jesus proved that people are more important than programs" and "Love is more important than rules." Agree or not? If this is true, what changes would need to be made in our families ... in our churches ... in our world?

Week 5

Upon This Rock
Matthew 16:13-20

Dear friends in Christ, grace, mercy, and peace, from God our Father and his Son, our Lord and Savior, Jesus Christ. Amen. The students were studying math in a fifth grade classroom, and the teacher was using the method of "estimating" to help them come to a greater understanding of numbers. "How many ping pong balls do you estimate there are in this jar?" she asked. "About how many do you think there are?"

One young boy estimated that there were forty. Another girl estimated 25. When the balls were taken out of the jar and counted, the correct number was forty, so the boy cheered for himself when he was given the prize. Then the teacher decided to ask how the students arrived at their answers. The little girl said, "Well, it looked like there were five balls on the bottom row, and there were five rows, so I counted up to five, five times." The boy who had the correct answer said, "Well, yesterday was my dad's birthday and he was forty, and that sounded like a good number." And which student was it that got the prize? Was it the one who thought and analyzed and estimated, though wrong? Or was it the one who took a flying leap at a number, and guessed correctly? Unfortunately, it was the one who guessed.

It seems to happen with regularity in our world: people who are perfectly willing to give an answer without thinking about the question. Even in religious circles, it happens. A pastor was giving a children's sermon one Sunday and began in this way: "Kids, what's small and gray and furry and climbs oak trees?" No response, so the pastor tried again: "Oh, come on, kids. It's small and furry, with a bushy tail, eats acorns and climbs oak trees." Finally, one little boy raised his hand. "Yes, Billy, do you know?" And Billy said, "Well, I was gonna say 'a squirrel' but I s'pose the answer's Jesus." Do you see what I mean? Giving an answer without thinking about the question, and it happens all the time in our world.

35

Our Lord had been with the disciples for quite some time, as this Gospel text opens up to us. They were with him long enough to watch him heal the lame. Long enough to watch him feed the 5,000. Long enough to see him walk on the water, and argue with the Pharisees, and teach the parables. So now the time had come for Jesus to do a reality check, to see if the disciples, or anyone else, had yet figured out who he was. So Jesus asked them plainly, "Who do people say that I am?" What do you hear on the streets? What are the people saying about me? Has anyone ventured a guess as to my identity, or my purpose, or the source of my authority?

The disciples must have recently discussed this very question, because their answers were immediate and specific. "Some people say you are John the Baptist. Others say you might be Elijah. Still others think you might be Jeremiah or one of the other prophets." They were listing their religious heroes, you see. They knew that Jesus spoke about God and that he was prophetic in nature, so they took a shortcut ... an estimate ... a guess, if you will.

But then Jesus made the question more pointed. "But who do you say that I am?" But who do you say that I am? It suddenly became obvious that Jesus was not content to hear what other people believed. He was not interested in public rhetoric or popular opinion, nor is he today. Jesus is always wanting to know what you think, or what you feel, or what you believe about him.

When Jesus made the question pointed and specific rather than vague and general, the disciples dared not say a word. No one dared to risk saying what he thought about Jesus. It was easier, after all, speaking for someone else. It was safer reporting what other people believed. So the disciples fell silent.

But not Peter. In an instant, Peter blended all that he knew about the man Jesus together with all that he knew about the promised Messiah. For a brief moment, the curtains raised, and he recognized who Jesus was. It was then that Peter blurted out his answer. "You are it! You are the Christ, the Son of the Living God!" If he was wrong, he would, at best, be humiliated ... and at worst, be stoned to death for blasphemy. But to Peter, it was worth the risk. Peter staked his opinion openly and boldly, and the other disciples stood there in awe.

The problem with the church today is that we are more like the other eleven disciples than we are like Peter. When we are asked to profess our faith, we spew out the religious words that we have heard in church over a lifetime, rarely stopping to think about their meaning. When we are asked to say what we believe, we describe what our parents believe, or mumble what we think our church believes, or report what popular culture says we're supposed to believe. What we are essentially doing is answering the first question of Jesus: "Who do people say that I am?" However, Jesus does not let us off the hook so easily. "But who do *you* say that I am?" Who *do* you say that he is?

Do you say that he is "Savior"? Do you know what that means? That means that Jesus and Jesus alone is responsible for dealing with your sins. Your good deeds have absolutely no power in earning forgiveness. Your guilt and shame cannot buy God off. Not even communion four times a month begets forgiveness; these elements are simply the reminder that if Jesus is Savior, your sins are no longer held against you. So please, don't just say he is Savior without thinking about it.

Who do you say that Jesus is? Do you say that he is "Lord" of your life: that makes you his servant. If he is the Lord, then you are the slave. It also means that everything you have is his, since slaves cannot own anything. Further, it means that whatever the master tells you to do, you have to do it. Have you ever thought about that?

Who do you say that Jesus is? Do you say that he is "Creator"? Is he Creator of everything? That means that he is creator of our enemies as well as our friends. He is the creator of people of different religions, people of different color. He is the creator of the people you love ... and the people you hate. Do you know what you are saying when you confess that Jesus is your Savior, and your Lord, and the Creator of the universe?

When Peter made his bold confession, Jesus bestowed upon him a most astonishing nickname. "You are Petros; I will call you a rock, because your faith is so solid." And then Jesus went on to say, "Upon this Rock I will build my Church." I respectfully take issue with our Roman Catholic brothers and sisters at this point.

Peter is not the Rock of the Church ... but his confession is. He was the first to confess Jesus as Lord. His statement of faith was the first stone in building a new Church that would come to worship the cornerstone ... Jesus Christ.

Well, the building of this Church has continued throughout human history, with each generation of Christians adding its stones of faith. Faithful people of every age have stood up and professed Jesus as their Savior and their Lord, and then they, too, became stones upon which the church is built. Saint Peter. Saint Paul. Saint Augustine. Martin Luther. Dietrich Bonhoeffer. Mother Teresa. It was not easy for them ... nor is it easy for us.

People, the time has come for each of us to stand up and be counted. Vague is no longer good enough. Lukewarm is no longer appropriate. Sincere confessions of faith are what the Savior asks of us, because the world needs to see bold, authentic witnesses once again. And not just the world, but our fellow church members, and our impressionable children, and our curious colleagues at work, and our weary friends and neighbors who wonder where the hope is in this world.

Tonight, you hold in your hands your contribution. It is a small stone, imperceptible perhaps, when compared to the mighty rocks that comprise the Church throughout history, but yours is every bit as important as theirs. For all the times we have failed to speak boldly about our faith in Jesus Christ ... for all the times we have denied ever knowing him ... for all the times we have withheld the possessions that we know belong to him — tonight we say we are sorry. And we lay our stone at the foot of the cross of Jesus Christ, and dare to be called his disciples. No power on earth can destroy what the Church has become. Thanks be to God. Amen.

Discussion Questions

1. If Jesus were to give you a "nickname" to describe your faith, what would it be, and why? (i.e. The Marshmallow, The Blaze, The Wimp, The Core) And what do you say about him?

2. Has there ever been a time in your life when "the curtains were opened up" and you had a clear view of Jesus, as Peter did? When did that happen? What did you see?

3. The other disciples were watching and listening when Peter pointed to Jesus as Messiah. Who has done that for you? Who, in your life, has pointed out Jesus as Savior and Lord? Have you ever told them that they did such a valuable thing?

Week 6

Crying Stones
Luke 19:29-40

Dear friends in Christ, grace, mercy, and peace, from God our Father and his Son, our Lord and Savior, Jesus Christ. Amen.

The journey has finally come to its illogical conclusion. After three years of teaching and preaching and helping and healing, Jesus tonight arrives in the city of Jerusalem, and there he is met by the screaming crowds. We've still a week to go in the season of Lent, but tonight marks the beginning of the end for Jesus.

It's the beginning of the end, but you wouldn't think so by listening to the people shouting out his name. "Jesus! Master! Jesus! Hosanna! Jesus! We love you!" As we shall hear this Sunday, the people actually threw their coats and jackets on the road for Jesus to walk upon; that's how excited they were. It was a parade ... a pageant ... a victory celebration of the first order. What contemporary illustration could possibly help us understand?

In 1987, we were living in Salem, Oregon, but in October of that year, I was scheduled to attend a conference back home in Minnesota. When my plane landed at about supper time, all four of my younger brothers were at the jetway to meet me, though I was expecting my parents to pick me up. "Where are Mom and Dad?" I asked, but my brother Jim said, "Never mind, we're going to the Metrodome!"

Just that afternoon, the Minnesota Twins had beaten the Tigers at Detroit for the American League pennant, and apparently the Molin boys were going to the victory party. We weren't alone! By the time we arrived, 55,000 fans had jammed into the stadium, and we only found places to stand at the very top row. For three hours, we screamed, we chanted, we spelled out "Twins" with our body parts: T-W-I-N-S. I had been transformed into a Twins fanatic and I didn't even live here anymore! And when the Twins players finally arrived, their bus rolled onto the playing field, and the Metrodome erupted! Everyone was screaming, laughing, crying, high-fiving, and hugging people we did not know. Our heroes had finally arrived!

And I think it must have been just this way in Jerusalem the day that Jesus arrived. People were laughing, crying, and hugging people they did not know, and all because Jesus the King had just ridden into town. What the people did not know is that the Pharisees were planning Jesus' demise. They were looking for a way to stop his mighty ministry, and when they found it, they would seize him. But what to do? What to do? His momentum was building; his popularity was growing by the hour. Something had to be done to quell the crowd.

Ever diplomatic, the Pharisees approached Jesus and asked him to settle down the raucous crowd. "Master, rebuke your disciples." That's what the text says. But behind their polite words and smiling faces, what they were really saying was, "Jesus, tell your people to shut up!" We can't have this noise. We can't continue this party atmosphere, for this ... this is the holy city of Jerusalem.

I love the Savior's response. "Tell the people to be quiet?" Jesus said, "Why, if I did that, then the stones on the street would start to cry out loud." You know, I wish he would have done it, just to see what cobblestones look like when they're screaming! But the point Jesus made is obvious; the emotion and the ecstasy of his entry into Jerusalem were so powerful, even the stones in the road could feel it. That kind of faith is contagious! That kind of faith is dangerous. That's why the Pharisees wanted it stopped ... and that is why Jesus would not tell the people to subdue their joy.

It seems to me that the world has been telling the disciples of Jesus to shut up ever since. Oh, they do this in the most subtle and seemingly innocuous ways, but the effect is still the same. The people of God are constantly told, "Settle down, don't be a fanatic, don't share the enthusiasm of your faith; in fact, don't even share your faith." It's offensive. It's politically incorrect. It's socially inappropriate. And we believe them. The result is that now our witness has been silenced, and our passion for Jesus is gone. Now we are lukewarm disciples ... no longer dangerous ... no longer a threat to anyone.

For ten years, I worked for the ministry called Young Life. For me, the highlight of that ministry was bringing young people to summer camp, at Castaway in northern Minnesota, or to one of the ranches in Colorado. Watching them grasp — watching them really understand — the gospel for the first time was amazing. And then to see them come to faith in Christ was such a privilege. On the last night of each week of camp, the youth are invited to participate in a "say so." That is, if they have committed their lives to Jesus Christ that week, they are invited to stand up in front of the whole camp and say so. Maybe the reason the say-so is so meaningful to me is because, in the summer of 1966, at Frontier Ranch in Colorado, I stood up and, for the first time in my life, announced that I believed in Jesus Christ. It was a defining moment in my life.

I mention this because one summer, I brought a young guy to camp and he stood up, too. He was so excited about this new faith, so on fire for Jesus Christ that he was dangerous. When he got home, the first person he told was his pastor, and do you know what his pastor said? "Oh, that's a bunch of nonsense! You've been baptized. You've been confirmed. You don't need any of that other stuff." Maybe that pastor was simply trying to be theologically correct, but what that young guy heard his pastor say was, "Shut up! We don't need this kind of noise around our church. It's better to keep your faith locked up inside." And that's sad.

So what's my point? It is this: we have listened to the voice of the Pharisees for too long. We have come to believe that God's grace is a private, personal matter, and it ought not to be expressed in public. At the same time, we tolerate immorality because it is not socially appropriate to make people accountable for their sins. Dr. Frank Harrington says it this way: "It's a little wink here, a little shrug there, a look the other way, and suddenly we find ourselves tolerating things and refusing to challenge behavior that is clearly wrong."[1]

I believe he is correct. We are afraid or ashamed to tell anyone that it is our faith that dictates how we live our lives. In short, Christians in general and Lutherans in particular have become silent about Jesus Christ. The world has told us to shut up, and we've said, "Okay." Well, shame on us! I am not suggesting that we become blatantly obnoxious; I am suggesting that we become publicly honest about our love for the Savior.

How many times have you and I had the opportunity to tell someone about God's forgiveness, and yet we remained silent? How frequently have we been tempted to say to someone, "I will pray for you," but instead we said nothing? How often do we consider inviting a colleague or a neighbor to church, but then chicken out at the last moment? You see, those are our sins of omission. The season of Lent is a good time to challenge those sins. But it calls us to make a choice ... to make a conscious decision not to be silent about news so great as this.

Tonight, may these stones stand for our sin of silence — the times we could have spoken a word of grace but did not. As we lay them at the cross of Christ, may our passion come alive. May our love for the Savior become known to all. Then the stones can be silent and we can sing praise. Thanks be to God. Amen.

---

1. Taken from *The Limits of Tolerance* by Dr. W. Frank Harrington, Peachtree Presbyterian Church, Atlanta, Georgia, January 10, 1999.

Discussion Questions

1. If Jesus rode into the parking lot of your work, or your school, or even this church, what kind of a reception would he receive?

2. Knowing what you do about Jesus, what differences are there between him and any earthly king? If you had been one of the Pharisees, do you think you would have recognized him as "King"?

3. In our world today, who is telling the followers of Jesus to shut up? Why do they do this?

Stones To Bread
Matthew 4:1-11

Dear friends in Christ, grace, mercy, and peace, from God our Father and his Son, our Lord and Savior, Jesus Christ. Amen.

Tonight is a night that is rich in tradition in the Christian Church. Those traditions vary greatly from congregation to congregation. Some churches this night focus on the poignant scene of Jesus washing the feet of his disciples on the night before he died, and they re-enact it. In full view of all worshipers, a husband might wash the feet of his wife, or a Sunday school teacher may wash the feet of her students, or perhaps the pastor would wash the feet of the church custodian and wipe them with a towel. The message becomes clear; humility and servanthood are the marks of the Christian Church, because they were the marks of Jesus Christ.

In another church, the focus of this night might be confession — honest, humble, and contrite confession. And not just because we are confessing our sins to God, but also by the confessing of our sins to each other.

It is the tradition among Christians in Africa on Maundy Thursday that, before the sacrament of Holy Communion is served, worshipers move about the sanctuary and seek forgiveness from everyone they have hurt or offended or sinned against — known or unknown — in recent months. It may take a few minutes; it might take an hour. But the service does not continue until every worshiper has been reconciled with every other worshiper. I have wondered how that would play in the North American Church, where grudges and gossip and secret sins are so prevalent among us. Frankly, I didn't have the courage for us to try it here.

In this church, a new tradition is beginning this evening. Young people, who have spent this Lenten season preparing to receive Communion, will receive it tonight for the very first time. I would to God that their anticipation and wonder — their sense of mystery and awe of this holy moment — I would to God that their joy

47

be contagious to us as we, too, hold in our hands tonight the very gift of God.

What all of these traditions seem to have in common, of course, is that they draw us near to Jesus on the night before he was crucified, and remind us that his love is the most powerful force this world has ever known. And not simply that we would *know* his love, but that we would *be* his love in this hurting world ... that we would *be* his servants in this self-serving world ... that *we* would personify his grace in this harsh and unforgiving world.

When the Apostle John was old and dying he was asked to bring one last message to the church. Slowly, haltingly, he stood before the congregation and said in a whisper, "Love one another." Then he was asked if there was anything else he would like to say. "Yes," John said. "Love one another." When the service had ended, his assistant asked him, "Brother John, why do you continue to repeat this same message?" And John replied, "Because if we would do this only, it would be enough." And that is the message we have come to receive from Jesus tonight: a new commandment that tells us to love. We will hear it. We will see it. We will eat it and drink it. And then we go from this place and we will be it.

Each Wednesday throughout this journey of Lent, we have carried small rocks into worship with us, and at the end of each service, we have laid them at the foot of that cross. People have complained to me that they didn't like it: that the stones were messy and left a chalky residue on their hands and clothing. It occurs to me that sin is like that: it's messy, it's unattractive, and it leaves its ugly mark upon our lives. That's the nature of sin. I don't know if you can see from where you are sitting, but the base of that cross is now covered by stones. Our stones. Our sins. They represent our hatred, and our gossip, and our pride, and our prejudice, and our failure, and our fear. Tonight, Jesus will do business with those stones.

As our Lord was beginning his public ministry, he spent forty days out in the middle of the Judean wilderness. Forty days — the same as Lent. At the end of that time, the Devil came to Jesus and tempted him.

"If you are the Son of God, command that these stones become bread." But Jesus answered and said, "It is written 'Man shall not live on bread alone, but on every word that proceeds out of the mouth of God.'"

Ironically, tonight Jesus *has* turned the stones to bread. Tonight, all the ugliness of our selfishness and sin is swallowed up by Jesus Christ. Now, the messy chalky residue of our sins stains not us ... they stain Jesus instead ... and we are left without a blemish. Tonight, you will not be handed a stone; tonight you will be handed a piece of bread and a promise. "This is my body, broken for you and for all the people, for the forgiveness of sin. Eat it and remember me." And now the stones are gone ... transcended by the Bread of Life.

If we are bewildered as to how this transaction happens, imagine the disciples on that first Maundy Thursday. They did not yet understand that the cross was just 24 hours away. They didn't have the slightest idea that in the span of one day, every one of them sitting at that table would bale out on their master. How clueless were they? They were still sitting at the dinner table when an argument broke out among them as to which of them was the greatest disciple! They didn't get it! If Jesus was ever going to withhold his gift of grace, that would have been the time! If Jesus was ever going to renege on his promise of forgiveness, that would have been it! But Jesus gave them the gift anyway.

You see, that's one of the great myths of this thing called "Holy Communion" — that we have to understand it before we can receive it. Do the fifth graders in our midst tonight know all there is to know about Communion? Are they now "qualified" to receive it? Or do you — after receiving the sacrament for twenty or thirty or forty years — now understand how it all works? Can you explain how something that looks like bread, and smells like bread, and feels like bread, and tastes like bread is actually the body of Jesus? I dare say, no, on all counts. All we *must* do is believe the promise of Jesus, and forgiveness is ours. That's why we call it "faith." The other myth about communion is that it's for the righteous. Well, the righteous don't need it; we do. Only we sinners need the gift that Jesus had to offer.

In a few moments, you will come forward to this rail, and you will kneel — if you can — and you will hold out your hands. You may hold a Ph.D. in quantum physics, but when you kneel at this rail, your hands will be empty. You may have a stock portfolio in the eight-figure range, but when you kneel at this rail, your hands will be empty. You may have a famous name, or a glamorous job, or a loving family, or loyal friends, or a notorious past, or a glorious future. But when you kneel at this rail, you are empty; and so am I. And the only thing that can fill our need tonight is bread.

I close with this: A young woman, who was a first-year student at Princeton Theological Seminary, was assigned to do her contextual education at a local nursing home. Every Wednesday, Janine would read scripture and pray prayers and serve communion to the elderly who would gather. And every one of the residents would gladly receive this gift of grace ... everyone, that is, except Madaline Jacks. Madaline never said a word to Janine during her visit. In fact, Madaline never said a word to anyone; she had stopped speaking years ago.

But one Wednesday afternoon, something happened. Something very, very special happened. As she did each week, Janine handed the wafer to Madaline, with the words, "The Body of Christ, Madaline, broken for you." But this week Madaline spoke. Holding the wafer between her thumb and forefinger, she smiled and said, "For me. Madaline Jacks. For me." And then she ate the Bread of Life.

Dear ones, tonight when you come forward with your broken hearts and empty hands and shattered dreams, may you know that Jesus has turned stones of sin into the Bread of Life. For you, the Body of Christ, for you. Thanks be to God. Amen.

Discussion Questions

1. If Jesus already knows our sins, why is it so important to confess them to God?

2. In what ways do "disciples" today compete with one another as to which is the greatest? How do you think God feels about this?

3. Is the concept of "emptiness" when going to the communion rail a new concept to you? How does this thinking of "emptiness" make you feel (i.e., humble, worthless, ashamed, in need)?

The Final Stone
Matthew 27:60

"It is finished." That's how John's Gospel records the closing moments in the earthly life of Jesus Christ. Each of the Gospel writers tells it a little bit differently, did you know that? Luke quotes Jesus as saying, "Father, into Thy hands I commit my Spirit," and then he died. Here in Matthew, Jesus cries out twice, "My God, my God, why have you forsaken me?" and then he died. In Mark, Jesus utters a loud cry and breathes his last breath. But I like John's version best. "It is finished." And then he died.

Now, none of these descriptions is inaccurate. When fear grips us and when sorrow overtakes us, each of us notices and remembers different things. But John makes a theological statement when he recalls Jesus' last words. "It is finished." What is *it*? *It* is the plan God crafted to bring humankind back into a secure relationship with the Father once again. *It* is the life project of Jesus, to allow himself to be sacrificed as the Lamb. *It* is the end of the most horrific week in human history, when loyalty and love was transcended by mob rule, and jealous hatred. *It*, explicitly, is the work of salvation. *It* was finished on Good Friday. In truth, *it* cannot be totally complete until you and I hear it, and see it, and grasp it, and own it as ours. And that is why this final stone is the most painful of them all. May God grant us faith and courage to ponder Good Friday, and the day *it* became God's gracious act.

Now, there are so many curious things to note in this tragic story of Jesus' death. The trial before Pilate was really a kangaroo court, because so many Roman and Jewish laws were broken in the process. For instance, the trial happened at night, while courts of justice were supposed to occur in the light of day. Jesus was convicted by a single judge, while typically a jury of three was required. The deliberations were supposed to go on for another day; it was society's way of "sleeping on it" before a man was sentenced to be executed. None of this was followed! But don't be too hard on the Roman and Jewish leaders of the day. "It" was supposed to be this way.

Ironically, if Jesus was to be executed for violating Jewish Law, he would not have been crucified, he would have been stoned to death; that was the Jew's way. Convicted criminals were brought to a pit at the edge of the city, pushed down the hill, and then stones would have been hurled at them until they stopped moving. In truth, this was a more humane practice, since death came so quickly. The Roman practice was much slower, much more painful, and much more hideous.

When a man was crucified, he was first stripped of his clothing and beaten. A "cat of nine tails" (a whip of leather, with pieces of sharp glass or stone at the end of it) was used across the back. Thirty-nine lashes were administered, because it was commonly thought that forty lashes would kill a man. They wanted him to be near-dead, so they could watch him die on the cross.

Then his naked body was laid across a timber on the ground, and nine-inch nails were driven through his wrists. He crossed his feet and a single nail pierced them. When the cross was righted and dropped into a hole, the flesh would often tear. And then the dying began. It took as long as six hours for the criminal to breathe his last. For a while, they could boost themselves up with their arms and legs. But as fatigue set in, their weary bodies slouched, their chest muscles caved in, and the windpipe was closed. Death was caused by suffocation.

According to *The Journal of the American Medical Association*:

> *Scourging produced deep stripes like lacerations and appreciable blood loss, and it probably set the stage for hypovolemic shock, as evidenced by the fact that Jesus was too weak to carry his own crossbar to Golgotha. Accordingly, death resulted primarily from shock and exhaustion asphyxia. Jesus' death was ensured by the thrust of a soldier's spear into his side.*[1]

When it was obvious that Jesus was dead, a Pharisee by the name of Joseph, a wealthy man, received permission from Pilate to take Jesus' body down from the cross on Friday night. The Jewish Sabbath was about to begin; if it were not done on Friday, it would have to wait until Saturday night. Joseph wanted to remove Jesus' body respectfully as soon as possible.

Scripture then says that Joseph brought Jesus' body and placed it in his own burial tomb. A large stone was rolled in front of the entrance of the grave, not only to close the grave respectfully, but also to prevent grave robbers from stealing Jesus' body and falsely proclaiming a resurrection. The stone, while we may picture it today as a large round boulder, was rather a large disk, set into a groove at the entrance to the grave, and then rolled into place after the body was inside. The resounding sound of its closing echoed the finality of Jesus' death: It is finished, indeed!

That is the historical evidence of Jesus' death. Though it is graphically ugly, we can keep it at a distance and it is not so difficult for us to consider. But the death of Jesus Christ was never intended to be taken historically ... or in a detached manner. It must be taken *personally*. And this is where Good Friday takes us ... to the foot of the cross ... to a grave loudly closed ... to a day without hope!

All the stones that you and I have laid at the foot of the cross this Lenten season have finally taken their toll. All the greed, all the hatred, all the vulgarity, all the selfishness, all the violence, all the unfaithfulness — they have not only covered the base of the cross, but they have littered our lives. And that's not even the sum total of our stones! We each have these secret sins, known only to us and God. God invites us to lay them at the cross as well. He takes them unto himself. The entire load, the enormous weight of them all, pressing down on his body as he hangs on the cross. Our stones. Our sins. His cross. And now, it is finished.

The final stone is the one which is rolled to the entrance of Jesus' grave. A final barrier, if you will, between us and the One who loved us so. When the final stone was rolled into place, it gave tangible expression to our sins. The sum of them is so enormous, they block us from God. They keep us from the kindest, loveliest man who ever lived. And hard as we may try, we cannot remove the stone ourselves. Not the stones at the base of that cross

... not the stone that seals Jesus' grave. Talk about feeling helpless! And that is exactly what we are! A helpless, hopeless people, partners in the Good Friday crucifixion of Jesus Christ.

You hold in your hands tonight, one final stone, too. This one is different from all the other stones of the season, for this one is marked with a black cross. It is also different in that we will not be leaving this stone in the sanctuary; rather, we will take it home with us. Let it be a reminder of the stones that keep us from loving God. Let it be a reminder of the stone that stands between us and a Savior. I implore you to carry it with you through the sorrow of tomorrow. Carry it with you through the anguish of Sunday's darkness. Perhaps bring it with you to worship on Sunday so that we may never forget the final stone that actually changed the course of human history. It is finished, indeed!

---

1. From "On the Physical Death of Jesus," *The Journal of the American Medical Association*, March 21, 1986.

Discussion Questions

1. What's "good" about Good Friday?

2. Honestly, which side would you have been on, if you had been at Calvary when Jesus was crucified? Would you have been one to cry, "Crucify him!" or would you have tried to defend him?

3. What's been one thing you have gained from this Journey of Stones?

He's Alive!
John 20:1-18

Dear friends in Christ, grace to you and peace — especially peace — from God the Father, and from his risen Son, Jesus Christ. Amen.

What a day! What a glorious, wonderful day! It is as if it were written in a Divine script; the sun is shining and the birds are singing and this sanctuary is dressed in a thousand different colors. It is Easter, friends: the One who was dead is now very much alive! I am reminded of the custodian who was cleaning the sanctuary after worship one Sunday, and noticed the pastor's sermon manuscript lying on the pulpit. Upon closer examination, he noticed that the pastor had written in large red letters in the left-hand margin: **Weak point! Raise voice and pound the pulpit!** I hope that's not what we're doing this morning. The disappointment of Good Friday has been replaced with unspeakable joy! Let's try this one more time: "He is risen!" *He is risen, indeed!* My prayer is that the truth of that single sentence will change your life ... today, tomorrow, and forever.

Now the story of our Lord's resurrection is told a bit differently in each of the four Gospels. In Matthew, two Marys went to the tomb early on Sunday morning to finish the painful task of embalming the body of the One they loved. In the Gospel of Mark, the Marys brought a woman named Salome with them. In Luke, the women are not identified at all by name, but still it was women — and not men — who first learned the Good News of Easter. I find that fact, in itself, quite fascinating.

But in John's Gospel, which we read today, Mary went to the grave all alone. Perhaps she went there to care lovingly for the body of Jesus, but more than likely, I think she went there to grieve. Most of the time, we need to be surrounded by family and friends when we are faced with the death of a loved one. Isn't that true? There is both comfort and strength in numbers. But sometimes, we don't want company. Sometimes, we just need to be alone; and I think this is the case with Mary on that first Easter Day. She needed some space; she just wanted time to mourn, and to wonder what might have been.

But curiously, when she arrived at the place where they had laid Jesus on Friday night, the large stone which sealed the entrance to the tomb was gone. Immediately, she jumped to a radical conclusion: grave robbers! She assumed that someone had stolen the body of Jesus, and she sprinted back to tell the others of her discovery.

But Peter and John were not content simply to *hear* about the news; when Mary told what she had discovered, they had to *go and see it* for themselves. They ran to the tomb. Out of fear, or curiosity, or anticipation, we don't know; but scripture tells us that they ran. John got there first, but he was a chicken! He saw the grave clothes but he wouldn't go inside, so he just sat there and waited for Peter. Peter, the impetuous one, didn't even break stride! He bolted into the grave, saw it was empty, and immediately knew that Jesus had risen from the dead. They didn't understand it all ... maybe they never did ... just like maybe we never do ... but they believed that Jesus was alive. Somehow, they knew that Jesus was alive. It seemed to suggest that we don't need to understand Easter to believe in the resurrection.

And I don't think it was just a coincidence that the first clue to the resurrection of Jesus Christ was that the stone had been removed. The theological implications are enormous! When Jesus was buried on Friday, a giant stone was placed between Jesus and the people who loved him. Though Mary went to visit Jesus' grave, she wouldn't be able to see him, because the stone was in the way. She wouldn't be able to touch him, because the stone would prevent her. It was like a barrier that she was incapable of moving herself. Somebody had to do that for her. And Somebody did.

Throughout the season of Lent, the members and friends of this congregation have been on what we called a "Journey of Stones." Each Wednesday, we would carry a small stone into worship with us, and that stone would become symbolic of our sins that are a barrier between us and God. After worship each Wednesday, we would lay our stones of sin at the foot of that cross. One stone stood for someone's pride, while another stone stood for someone's dishonesty. One stone symbolized a couple's fractured marriage, while other stones stood for the sins of gossip, or prejudice, or adultery, or hatred. By the end of Lent, the base of the cross was filled with stones. Our stones. Our sins. We can't remove those sins by ourselves; someone has to do it for us. And Someone has. Maybe you can't see the base of that cross this morning, but I can, and I tell you that it's empty! All the stones are gone. All the sins are removed. And that is the ultimate message of Easter: that what we could not do by ourselves, God did for us, no questions asked.

Every pastor knows that on Easter Sunday, he or she is preaching to people who may not be regular worshipers. Perhaps some of you are in worship today for the first time in years ... perhaps some for the first time ever. You have sins, yes? You drink too much, or you swear too much, or you are angry too often, or you have been unfaithful in too many relationships. And maybe that is even the reason you have stayed away from church: your shame has been too much for you to overcome. In truth, you are no different than the rest of us. Today it is my privilege to tell you that the stone has been rolled away for you, too. You may think that your sins are too great to be forgiven, but you're wrong. You may think that God can't accept you just the way you are, but you're wrong. The stone is rolled away! The sins have been forgiven. The Savior has chosen to love you.

There is a story about W. C. Fields, the famous vaudeville comedian, who was also a notorious atheist. One evening, before his performance, an assistant came into Fields' dressing room and caught Fields reading a Bible. Embarrassed, Fields slammed the Bible shut and said, "Just looking for loopholes!" What Fields was looking for is grace. What he was looking for is forgiveness ... a second chance ... a time to start over. Well, Easter is the ultimate loophole! When Jesus made good on his promise to raise from the grave, all of his promises became reality. His promise to forgive sins. His promise to be with us wherever we would go. His promise to give us eternal life. That's no loophole; that's a fact!

Today we are surrounded by the evidence of Easter. The flowers, the hymns, the confident voices of our friends who boldly claim, "He is risen ... risen indeed!" It's easy to believe in the resurrection today ... but what about tomorrow? What about Tuesday, or next Saturday, or later on in May? What about when people let us down ... or when loved ones die ... or when the sins of our lives overwhelm us once again? Will Easter then be just a distant memory? How will we believe then?

In 1988, when the Berlin Wall came tumbling down, a young woman named Anna in East Germany was already asleep when her friend pounded on the door. "Anna, the Wall is down, and we have freedom!" she said. "You must come and see!" They ran down to the gate that had divided east and west for thirty years, and it *was* true. The Berlin Wall had been toppled. For three hours they partied on the border. They ran back and forth between east and west, they drank beer and danced with soldiers. Then they went back to their homes.

The next morning, Anna awoke and thought she had dreamed that experience; it all seemed too good to be true. Quickly, she got dressed and ran back down to the border and remembered that it was all true. But this time, before she went back home, she picked up a shattered piece of the Berlin Wall and took it home with her, now a tangible reminder that she was free.

As you leave today, you too, will be given a reminder that you are free. A prayer pebble marked with the word "Alive" will be handed to you. May it be for you a reminder that you are free. May it be a reminder that you are released from the shame of your sins. Free from the punishment of God. Free to be alive! And if the Son makes you free, you shall be free, indeed. Happy Easter, my friends. Thanks be to God. Amen.

CPSIA information can be obtained
at www.ICGtesting.com
Printed in the USA
LVOW04s0030030216

473445LV00023B/140/P